Thailand

Your Ultimate Guide to Traveling, Culture, History, Food and More!

Experience Everything Travel Guide Collection™

Forward

Thank you for purchasing this book from the Experience Everything Travel Guide Collection™! Inside you will find a ton of useful, informative and entertaining information on Thailand and it is our desire that this book will provide you with the inspiration to explore!

Disclaimer

While this book contains a great deal of information, it does not have all of the information that is available on the Internet. It is written to inspire you about the destination rather than act as a full travel guide that you could use to get from point A to point B or to specific addresses/locations during your tour.

Contents:

Chapter I: Introduction and Geography

Thailand is a beautiful country comprised of 76 provinces. You will find it situated in Southeast Asia, just in the center of the Indochina peninsula. Tourists flock Thailand each year for its beautiful beaches, simple way of life, rich history and culture as well as its friendly people.

The national animal of the country and its symbol is the elephant. In 1850, there were about 100,000 elephants being domesticated in Thailand. However, the numbers dropped as the years went by. This is due to elephant poaching wherein their ivories, hinds and meat have been very attractive to hunters. In modern, Thailand anti-poaching measures have been introduced and there are even elephant sanctuaries.

The country is lying on the east of Cambodia and Laos. On its south lies Malaysia and the Gulf of Thailand. Meanwhile, Burma borders the country to its north while the Andaman Sea is found to its west.

Bangkok is the capital city of the country. It is also the most populated and is a popular gateway for foreigners wanting to visit Thailand. It is also the center of trade and commerce, politics and other cultural activities. Other parts of the country are divided into villages and districts.

Nonthaburi is the second largest municipality in Thailand having more than 260,000 population. It is followed by Pak Kret and Hat Yai from the provinces of Nonthaburi and Songkhla. The municipality of Nakhon Ratchasima is the fifth largest in the country holding more than 135,000 of residents.

The country runs under a constitutional monarchy government. It is under the leadership of the Royal Family where the King Bhumibol Adulyadej stands as the leader of the state. He has been in power for more than half a decade making him the longest king to hold power in the Thai kingdom. The main religion in the country is Buddhism although there are also other growing sectors in Thailand.

Climate

Thailand embraces tropical climate which attracts westerners and other visitors from neighboring Asian countries. The country is best known for its hospitable people and its diversified culture. This has made international guests pick Thailand for their next tour in Asia. The kingdom never runs out of fascinating activities and hot spots to visit.

The seasons in the country has been divided by region. Northern Bangkok experiences three seasons while the peninsular region in southern Thailand only experience two. Mostly throughout the year, the country is humid and tropical.

Meanwhile, the northern part of the country has a well defined season. If you are planning to visit sometime between November to February, you may experience dry weather. By March to May, higher temperatures are experienced. The northern part of Thailand are also not affected by the northeast monsoon although it does bring about cool breezes. By May to November, Thailand's northern part experience heavy rain caused by the southwest monsoon.

On the other hand, Thailand's southern region experience only two seasons which do not fall on the same time with the east and west side of the country. The west experiences heavy storms due to the southwest monsoon by April to October. Meanwhile, heavy rain occurs from September to December on the east coast.

This would mean that the country's southern parts experience heavy rains about 2,400 millimeters annually while the northern and central parts of Thailand experience about 1,400 millimeters of rain each year.

Language

The primary language in the country is Thai although English is widely used and understood by locals especially in Bangkok. Meanwhile, European languages are also spoken in major restaurants, shops and hotels as well as in other tourist areas. Visitors will have no worries getting around Thailand as road signs have Thai-English descriptions written on it.

The traditional greeting of Thailand, wai,, is offered by the younger person whenever he meets another person. Hands are being pressed together with the fingertips pointing above. Then the head is bowed wherein the face should touch the fingertips while saying "sawatdi khrap" for boys and "sawatdi kha" for girls. Older people will respond in the same way after the younger ones made their greetings. The wai greeting symbolizes respect that can be likened to the namaste greetings of India and Nepal.

Religion

About 90% of Thais are mostly Theravada Buddhism practitioners. This is also the national religion of the country. Thailand is also among the strong believers of Buddhism, joining other Buddhist countries in the world. Meanwhile, there are also other sectors in Thailand practicing other faiths. This include Christianity, Hinduism and Islam and all other sects that are allowed freedom of worship. However, Buddhism still dominates the country with influences stretching forth to the daily lives of people.

Thais revere their senior monks highly. That is why you would mostly see a temple built in the center of a town or village. A common practice among Buddhists in Thailand is meditation. They believe that this promotes inner peace and happiness making it a regular practice among them. Visitors are also welcome to learn the fundamentals of meditation found in Bangkok or in other places across Thailand.

There are a lot of immigrants working and living in Thailand for a number of years. This included skilled workers like artists, musicians, writers, sculptors, dancers and architects who have helped locals to boost their culture.

Today, people in Thailand share a broad ethnic diversity. They are the Thais, Malays, Persians, Chinese, Khmer, Mon and the Indians. Because of this, you will not be able to distinguish the typical physique of a local as some are tall while other as petite. Some have round faces, others have dark skin while others are light-skinned.

Education

The literacy rate in the country is at 93.5% according to a data gathered in 2014. This makes the education system of Thailand well-rounded. Students attend kindergarten, primary school followed by the lower and secondary schools. Numerous vocational schools and universities are also found in the country. Meanwhile, the government mandated compulsory education for every child until the age of 14.

Industry

The primary livelihood in the country is agriculture followed by tourism. Between 1985 to 1996, the country experienced fast growth in their economy. They also ranked second in terms of quality of life among the 10 ASEAN countries. Thais are also influenced by ceremonies and religious festivities making it distinct among other nations in South East Asia.

Aside from its booming tourism industry, Thai cuisine is also a favorite among visitors. It is widely known for its five blended flavors including sweet, spicy, salty, bitter and sour. Thai food has been influenced greatly by the Chinese especially when it comes to noodles and soups.

Chapter II: Thailand History

The name of the country was derived from the Thais, the dominant ethnic group in Thailand. The Kingdom was never under a European colony. However, it was under absolute monarchy until its government shifted to constitutional monarchy in 1932.

By 1939, the country also changed its name from Siam to Thailand where military dictators held leadership until the earl 70s. They were still holding power and influenced politics until the early 90s. By 1997, a new constitution was adopted by Thailand. This resulted to the diminishing role of the military in the country's political scene.

Thailand's military governments started promoting rapid economic growth after World War II ceased. They also tried to get rid of ethnic minorities. The boost in the economic situation in Thailand continued until the latter part of the 1990s. Meanwhile, more liberal policies were adopted and directed towards ethnic minorities under the ruling of the 1990 democratic government. On the other hand, ethnic minority members were confronted with numerous issues especially when it comes to their economic security and political rights.

Bangkok became the capital of the country replacing Ayutthaya in the late 18th century. This was after invaders from Burma sacked Ayutthaya in 1767. Currently, Bangkok is the central and most important city in terms of politics, trade and other economic undertakings. The capital holds about 10 million population while twenty smaller cities in the region have residents of about two hundred thousand to three hundred thousand.

The northeastern part of the country holds great evidence that it was once an agricultural civilization. Bronze artifacts were also found about 3000 years ago in the same part of the country. During the 8th and 9th centuries, Indian civilization greatly influenced the CE Mon states which occupied parts of the northern and central parts of the kingdom.

From then, a number of Tai-speaking immigrants began coming in Thailand. These people were from Vietnam and Yunnan who had contacted the Mons in the country. They were able to convert a large number of Mons to Theravada Buddhism.

As the Khmer empire began its expansion, Tai peoples also started occupying central Thailand. The Tais were then referred to as Siams who rebelled against the Khmer regime in 1238. The revolt resulted to a writing system which later on became Thailand's basis of governance.

By the time the Khmer regime declined in power, central Thailand's power was shifted to the southern parts of the country up to the Ayutthaya, established in 1351. Meanwhile, the northern kingdom of Lan Na was established 1259 while the kingdom of Lao of Lan Sang was established in 1353.

At the later part of the 15th century, Ayutthaya and Lan Na were strong and affluent states. However, the kingdoms degenerated after the deaths of their respective rulers. During the 16th century, Ayutthaya was attacked by Burmese people and the Khmers. It was in 1585 that Ayutthaya started to rejuvenate. By 1511, a Portuguese embassy was established in the kingdom which contributed to the growing European presence in Thailand. However, the country was once again invaded by the Burmese in 1765 and was later on captured and destroyed by 1767.

Meanwhile, a new capital in Thonburi was established after defeating the Burmese invaders. In 1782, Chao Phraya Chakkri was crowned king and later on established Bangkok. The king also founded the royal title system and called himself Rama III. It was also during his time that a number of treaties were signed among European countries and the United States. Missionaries were also allowed to enter the kingdom in pursuit of propagating Christianity.

In 1932, Thailand's form of governance was shifted and became constitutional monarchy. This was after a group of young Thais scholars initiated a coup. Military dictator Phibun ruled the country from 1935 until 1945. He was also responsible in changing the name Siam to Thailand. By

1945, the country briefly returned to the civilian government wherein its name was changed back to Siam.

Different military dictators ruled Thailand from 1947 to 1973. The military was forced to leave office after the rampant suppression of demonstrators who rallied against the government. However, by 1976, the military was able to regain control over Thailand.

After four years, Prem Tinsulanonda led a more moderate form of governance after he assumed office. Prem was also cited to have delivered Thailand into having a stable economy as well as a stabilized political scene. This was also the time wherein Thailand experienced a slow transition to democracy from communist insurgency. By 1988, new set of government officials were placed into office but was later removed after a military coup was held in 1991.

By 1991, a new constitution was made an another election was held a year after. The country was then returned to civilian governance. Thailand experienced long periods of political and economic instability. It was only in 1997 that the country made a democratic reformist constitution. By early 2001, national elections were called under the newly promulgated constitution.

Chapter III: Thailand Culture

The culture in Thailand was greatly influenced by the Tais. It was during the time of military dictator Phibun that a number of cultural rules were enacted. These mandates included promotion of identity and centralized national culture. It was also included that a national language should be followed as well as the use of the country's national dress.

Thailand's then military government wanted to ensure that the country remained to have its culture inculcated in the coming generations. This was to avoid western culture to highly influence the Thais. The Ministry of Education of the country also played a big role in disseminating cultural information. By 1979, a commission directed towards national culture was established.

Local and regional identities started to revive by the 1980s. It was during this time that local foods, numerous styles of traditional dress and festivities resurged in the northern and northeastern part of the country. The process was further allowed to accelerate after reforms leading towards democracy were made by the 1990s.

Class

Thailand also classified its people according to a social strata by the 19the century up to the early part of the 20th century. The upper class comprised of the Thai elites while the middle class was made up of European and Chinese businessmen. Meanwhile, rural farmers formed the lower class of the system.

The system has transformed into a more complex class following the growth of the modern economy. Those who are born as nobles have some position in the society although wealth is the primary basis of the modern class system. The middle class has also grown but the lower class has grown even more following the growth of the urban poor in addition to the traditional farmers from the rural areas.

The division of labor is not rigidly followed in Thailand. Both men and women perform agricultural workload. However, a variation of work in some regions is observed. In northern Thailand, it is a man's duty to plow the land and sow seeds while in the central, women also do the task.

Domestic work is done by women as well as weaving, basketry, making umbrellas, pottery and lacquerware manufacturing. Gender inequality can be seen through discrimination, violence and even human trafficking. More efforts to promote equality has been made by 1997 when the constitution mandated providing women with protection and equal rights.

Marriage

Marriage in Thailand is a part of the traditional culture. Fix marriages have not been observed although individuals are usually influenced to marry those who are wealthy. You will be able to recognize a wealthy couple getting married by the kind of ceremony they have. Having more than one wife has been rampant among the elite in the past decades. However, it has now become uncommon. Divorce is also difficult especially when couples ended up fighting with regards to property division.

Ideally, married Thais should have their own household. However, those who are in the poor classes remain with either their husband or wife's family after marriage. Thai families also observed extended family units that include siblings who are not yet married and widowed parents. The husband serves as the head of the family although the wife is also an important authority.

Chapter IV: Modes of Transportation

Skytrain

Getting around Thailand is not a problem because there are different types of available transportation available in the country. Most people make use of the main transport system, the Skytrain. It is convenient because it links one popular tourist spot to another. The Skytrain operates above the streets. A passenger should go up several floors to be able to get a train ride. It is important to carry change with you as the ticket system would have you pay between 5 to 10 baht coins. In case you haven't got change, you can always go to a BTS counter to have your bills exchanged to coins. Before you can make a purchase, the ticket system will ask which station you want to go. After which, you have to put your coins inside the slot followed by the ticket for the train ride. If you don't want to go to the hassle of purchasing tickets on the exact time of your travel, you can always purchase a ticket a day ahead. Tourists should also remember that a Skytrain fare is different from a subway ticket.

Private Car

In Phuket, transportation has been an issue among travelers. This is why most of them rent a private car along with the services of a driver for a day's tour. This is more convenient as you are allowed to make your own schedule and the places where you want to visit. Drivers in rent-a-car services in Phuket usually speaks good English making a tour even more convenient.

Taxis

Metered taxis are another transportation option. You can get int a yellow can from the airport to your hotel or any place within the Phuket town. However, you have to remember that some drivers drive really fast and that you have to brace yourself for a ride. Local buses are also available in Phuket wherein you have to pay about 30 baht per ride.

Train

Most travelers think that the best way to get to Chiang Mai from Bangkok is by taking a plane ride. However, the best choice so far is by taking an overnight train. It is safe, clean and will offer you a fun and comfortable experience. Families can take the first class cabin while those who are traveling alone can share a cabin in the second class. However, the restroom is shared in the second class cabins and that it can get noisy when other people want to talk and drink. Meanwhile, the restrooms in the first class cabins are only shared by a number of passengers.

Train food can be a little costly. A waiter will take your orders from the cabin and deliver the food thereafter. You can also place your order for breakfast ahead of time and tell the waiter the time you want it delivered.

Overnight trains with first class accommodation leave Bangkok for Chiang Mai at 6 PM. They will arrive the designated spot the following day at about 7 AM. The trains are popular among tourists making tickets sell like hot cake. It is important that you have a prior booking as you can buy tickets even 60 days before your desired trip.

Tuk-tuks

The tuk-tuks or sam-lor are also a popular mode of transportation in Thailand. These are actually auto rickshaws having three wheels that operates within different Thai cities. The tuk-tuks are also popular causes of heavy traffics especially in Nakhon Ratchasima and Bangkok.

Minibuses and Motorbike Taxis

Meanwhile, travelers should be cautious about going around Pattaya between 7:00 AM to 9:00 AM and from 3:00 PM to 6:30 PM. This is when traffic gets congested and hold-ups happen in major roads. The traffic condition gets even worse during heavy rains and after a downpour. Unlike other cities in Thailand, there are no tuk-tuks in Pattaya. Travelers can get in minibuses and motorbike taxis instead. The songthaews operate around

Pattaya and can cost 10 baht per ride. These baht buses can also take you to routes wherein you need to pay a little extra.

Scooters

When in Ko Samui, you can always rent a motorbike or scooter to get around the island. The cost starts from 250 baht for a day's rent available in different rental companies. However, some hotels offer scooter rentals for added convenience to guests. Owners don't usually ask to see if you have an international driving license. The first question they would ask you is if you have driven a motorbike before.

Renters should take note that not all companies provide bike rental insurance. This is means that the insurance you've paid back home can only cover for the car or jeepney ride you take. This would also mean that you have to ride at your own risk when renting motorbikes and scooters. Before you get on a rented bike, be sure to have pictures of it taken and check on damages so you won't be charged for breaking or scratching the vehicle. Gas is available in most shops situated along the streets. You can buy a liter for 40 baht while a full tank can get you charged with 80 baht.

Ferries

On the other hand, travelers going to Krabi from Ko Samui can get into a ferry ride costing 500 baht. There are different travel agencies offering the service that comes with free hotel pickup. A ferry, pretty much looking ancient but in good condition, in Nathon will take you to Dousak. The trip would embark about after 8 AM and would arrive Dousak half past nine in the morning. From there, you need to take a bus ride bound for Krabi.

Boats

Another mode of transportation to try is the boats of Khlong Express. The experience would be worth while after barreling through the narrow canals of Bangkok. Take note of the heavy noise along the way. Those who are faint hearted should not get on this ride as you will need an extra hand to pull you up after.

Walking

Meanwhile, some travelers love to explore places around the cities of Thailand by walking. This is also an exciting way to get yourself transported from one place to another without the hassle of going up and down from a bus. You can also enjoy the sights that you come across and conveniently take pictures when possible. Walking can also have you stop to buy street foods compared to taking a ride wherein you have to wait until the bus

comes to a nearest stop.

Chapter V: Where to Stay while in Thailand

There are 10 cities in Thailand and 14 other tourists destinations. These cities include Bangkok, Ayutthaya, Chiang Mai, Chumphon, Chiang Rai, Kanchanburi, Nakhon Ratchasima, Pattaya, Sukhothai and Surat Thani. Meanwhile, other destinations include Ko Chang, Ko Lipe, Ko Pha Ngan, Ko Samet, Ko Samui, Ko Tao, Khao Lak, Khao Sok National Park, Khao Yai National Park, Krabi Province, Phuket, Khon Kaen, Mae Sot and Mae Sariang.

The country's tourism industry has been booming and finding a hotel to book your Thailand vacation is not difficult. There are a lot of sources available from travel magazines, online and even from your relatives and friends who have already visited the country. Reading customer reviews about a hotel, a pensione house or a budget inn will always be helpful to select the best place to comfortably stay in.

Bangkok

Bangkok is a busy city. It is best to choose a hotel near the Skytrain to be able to get close to the places around the city. You can book a reservation with Glow Trinity Hotel or Lebua at State Tower in Silom. This area is best known for its shopping and business centers. It is also close to the route of the Skytrain and the nightlife in Patpong. The room rates in Glow Hotel starts from around $60 for a deluxe room going up to $90 for a premier deluxe room booking. Meanwhile, Lebua at State Tower offers $115 per night for a superior suite balcony room and as much as $300 per night for a river view suite accommodation.

Travelers can also have a hotel booked at the Tai Pan Hotel for a cheap rate of $44 per night. Most of these rooms have optional breakfast inclusion offered at an extra price. The Dynasty Grand Nana Hotel in Bangkok is also an excellent choice for those who want to stay near bars and GoGos. Room rates start from $68 per night with a choice of either smoking or non-smoking rooms.

Another hotel recommended for travelers is the Ibis Nana Hotel. You get to pay $44 per night for a standard double room. Restaurants are all over the hotel so you won't find yourself getting hungry even during late nights or the wee hours of morning. If you want to relax and unwind, Navalai River Resort is also an excellent choice. The hotel is situated in Riverside Bangkok and has a very serene ambiance. The rates start from $50 per night for a serene double room accommodation.

Other options while in Bangkok also include Peninsula Bangkok Hotel, Ramada Plaza Bangkok Menam Riverside, Mandarin Oriental Hotel, Best Western Premier Amaranth Suvarnabhumi Airport, Novotel Bangkok Suvarnabhumi Airport and the Regent Suvarnabhumi Hotel.

Phuket

Meanwhile, visitors traveling to Phuket should choose the hotel where they plan to stay because they might end up getting an accommodation too far from the hot spots since the island is about 20 kilometers wide and 50 kilometers long. Most travelers chose to stay near Patong because there are a lot of shopping areas, party places, markets and bars located in that area. Meanwhile, those who love the nightlife can book a hotel in Bangla Road.

Some hotels in Phuket to choose from include Royal Paradise Hotel, Millennium Resort Phuket, Thara Patong Beach Resort & Spa, Royal Crown Hotel, The Surin, Indigo Pearl, Anantara Villas, Club Bamboo Boutique Resort & Spa and the Avantika Boutique Hotel.

The Marriott Hotel in Phuket is situated just 15 kilometers north from the airport. The room rates start from 7,000 baht per night and is best for families and couples. Another place to stay while in Phuket is the Kamala Beach Estate located in the southernmost part of the Kamala Beach. The rates vary according to season with the lowest season price of 9,900 baht for a 3 bedroom villa. During peak seasons, the price increases to more than 15,000 baht for a bedroom villa. For those who are on a budget, Rome Place Hotel is a good choice. It is situated near Phuket bus station and is only 30 minutes away from famous beaches in the island.

Pattaya

Those who want to stay Pattaya will have no problem getting around the city as minibuses are widely available. The city offers nightlife which is mostly sought after by foreigners aside from its wonderful beaches. While in Pattaya, you can book a stay with Marriott Hotel, Tim Hotel, Dusit D2 Baraquda, the Rabbit Resort, Areca Lodge, Hotel Idyll, Camelot Hotel and the Aya Boutique Hotel, a modern style hotel built within the heart of Pattaya City.

You can also check accommodations at LK Metropole and the Sunbeam Hotel. Holiday Inn also offers great accommodation. You can choose from more than 500 guestrooms that offers a great view of the ocean from their window. Take note that these suggested hotels vary in prices and accommodations.

Chiang Mai

Chiang Mai is the country's original capital city dated back in history. The city offers great architecture and a rich history. It is also beautifully situated among the hills found the northern part of Thailand. Travelers who plan to spend their vacation in Chiang Mai are mostly indulged in escaping busy tourist spots within Thailand. The city is best known for its scenic beaches and first class hotel accommodations. These hotels include Four Seasons Resort and the Chedi

Chiang Mai. Other hotels found in Chiang Mai are De Naga Hotel and Amora Tapae Hotel.

Krabi

Krabi is the gateway for some scenic beaches although the city itself is a working zone. Travelers take a stop in Krabi because it is cheaper to book an accommodation there rather than going directly to a nearby beach. There are also other scenic beaches near Krabi that visitors can go directly to. For instance, the Ao Nang Beach Resort is just 20 kilometers away by car from the city.

Meanwhile, visitors can take a pick from a number of hotels in the city. This includes accommodation from Villa 360 Resort, Cabana Hotel, Phra Nang Inn and Ao Nang Villa. You can also inquire for room rates and amenities at Railay Village Resort, Phi Phi Banya Villa and the Railay Bay Resort.

If this is your first time to travel to Thailand, remember to have a prior booking to ensure that there is a room waiting for you when you arrive. This will save you the time and hassle from moving to one place from another in search of a place to stay. Some travel agencies offer discounts for advance bookings that can save you a lot of money. There are cheap guesthouses found all over Thailand while those who want to spend for a luxurious stay can book with a $10,000 per night accommodation.

Chapter VI: Where to Go and What to Eat

There are five culinary regions on the country. This include the northeastern region, the north, the central part, the south and Bangkok. These regions have their distinct style in cooking according to the taste of locals and the available ingredients in every place. Having a taste of every recipe in various regions will get you a feel for the entire cooking in the country as a whole. Some travelers prefer to have a taste in the culinary offerings of a region to determine the best places to visit. This can be true as traveling and food are somewhat related. Of course, you would not want to stay in a place that offers limited good food.

Northern Region

The northern part of Thailand including Chiang Mai has been existing as a separate kingdom until the 1800s. It is safely situated in a fortress of trees, rivers and mountains. Because the region is isolated, the people living there has also developed their own dialect. Aside from this, they have also developed a unique style when it comes to cooking.

Thailand's northern part has no coconuts compared to the south where coconut milk flourish. Sticky rice is a staple food to pair spicy dishes in this region compared to other places where it is eaten as dessert.

Vegetarian restaurants have also become abundant in the region although most of the food is based mainly on red meat. The recent infusion of vegetables in the city was due to the focus of wellbeing and the promotion of peace. Restaurants have been gaining popularity due to its use of organic products. You can try Thai Jungle Curry or the spicy Lettuce wraps.

Northeastern Region

Meanwhile, the northeast region of Thailand has been stricken with poverty. Massive droughts are common especially during summer seasons. Fish and coconut milk are scarce similar to the north. When animals are being cooked, Thais in the northeast region leave no waste. This means that they include the tongue, intestines, liver and heart when they cook. Broiling as well as roasting has been the common cooking style. The most common dish in the region is having sticky rice paired with green papaya salad.

In the southern region, beaches can be found lying peacefully along the coast on white sand beaches. It is abundant with palm trees while the peninsula has long mountain ranges stretching from the north to the south. The region joins Malaysia through its long peninsula. Making tourists get attracted to visiting the island as many islands can be found in the south of Thailand including the famous Phuket island.

Southern Region

The main industry in the south is fishing where fish sauce production has been in large scale. Fish sauce has been seen to be an important ingredient in most Thai dishes. The southern region offers travelers abundant fish and seafood dishes. This is because of the abundance in fish in the area. Coconuts are also flourishing in the south making coconut milk based curries served in mostly all restaurants in the southern region. Fresh tropical fruits including papaya, pineapple, mango and mangosteen make up of the southern region desserts.

Central Plains

Meanwhile, the central plains of Thailand is regarded as Asia'a great rice bowls. It is also the heart of the country where rice farms are flourishing. However, the region experience floods during the monsoon season as it was a swamp before. Noodles made from rice are usually served for lunch or snacks. The abundance of water in the central plains make it easier to grow rice. In fact, this is the region where jasmine scented rice is planted, harvested and exported all over the world.

The central plains offer its visitors the popular Pad Thai with various flavors including fish, chicken and beef. Desserts are mostly made from banana and mango.

Bangkok Area

Bangkok has been regarded to have a lot of restaurants. In fact, most people say that it has a number of restaurants found per square mile of the city than anywhere else you can visit. The city seems to operate due to its busy food industry. You will be able to find a hefty number of eateries and street food kiosks as long as fast food stalls. Thai fast food usually serves spring rolls, fish cakes, satay sticks and a lot more.

The capital is also known to have a lot of dishes coming from different parts of the country being served to visitors. The presence of the Chinese people in Bangkok has greatly influenced their cooking method. Traditional Chinese meals have been given a touch of Thai cooking making their versions of the stir fried dishes, noodles, sweet and sour dishes and a lot more.

Another form of cooking present in Bangkok is the palace style cooking method. The method of preparing the dish is more intricate especially that vegetables are being cut meticulously and flavors are more refined compared to regular home style cooking. The presentation of the dish is intricately done with carved vegetables turned into flowers and are included withing the dish.

Thai dessert is a must try when in Bangkok. You will be able to soothe your taste buds from a hefty number of choices including jellies, cakes and puddings. These are mostly made from rice, egg, sugar and coconut base. Desserts also vary in cooking style as the palace method is more refined while others may seem to look repugnant.

Bangkok is also known for its street food. You can get a noodle soup for less than $2 while fish cakes will cost you only less than $1. Authentic street food are abundant in China where visitors usually dig in various dishes. You can try on dumplings and the special oyster omelet to complete your Chinatown dining experience.

The busy Silom Road is also an excellent choice if you want to get your stomach full with street food. As the business district is filled with busy and hungry people, you will find an abundance of street food stalls scattered all over. Cheap yet delicious street food is mostly found in Soi 20 and Soi Convent.

Soi Rambutti is also a popular destination for those who want to escape the fast paced life in Bangkok. Wee hour treats are served on this street, suitable after you have indulged in night alley shopping.

Types of Food in Thailand

Thailand has been regarded the land of smiles and it isn't a surprise as Thais are cheerful and happy go lucky natives. Backpackers often choose the country due to its beautiful beaches and great food. The climate is also magnificent, making you enjoy the sun in the tropics. However, it is their delicious food that entices people to come to the country. Aside from the fact that it's delicious, you won't get your pockets ripped as these are also very affordable.

The most sought after food in the country is the Pad Thai. It is comparable to Chinese and Japanese noodles with a different taste. It is found mostly anywhere in the streets of Thailand as well as in restaurants all over the country. It is made with meat,tofu, egg, rice noodles and vegetables. Vendors have it stir fried in a small wok and complete the dish with spices and sauces.

Another must try while in Thailand is the Som Tam or the papaya salad. It is a refreshing dish and probably the easiest Thai food to prepare. The ingredients include fish sauce, chili, lemon juice and sweet palm. These are placed in a big mortar and are crushed until thoroughly mixed. The dominant flavors include sweet and sour. The papaya salad is prepared in front of buyers making you sure of what's inside the food you are about to eat.

As there are plenty of available Thai food found along the streets and in restaurants, you have to indulge yourself in a bowl of Tom Yam Goong. This dish is made with chili, keffir lime leaves and lemon grass. The fragrant herbs create such aroma that you would want to ask for more. You can also choose from chicken or fish to be added to your Tom Yam Goong bowl. Meanwhile, you can also have tofu, straw mushrooms and prawns as meat alternative. Take note that this spicy and you might end up drinking more glasses of water.

The Green Curry or Geng Kheaw Wan is also a favorite among curry lovers. It has a specific aroma that will make you remember you have visited Thailand. Unlike the spicy red curry, the green curry is sweet. It is made with lemon grass for the green curry paste, bamboo shoots, aubergine, fish sauce and garangal. Meanwhile, vegetarians can substitute meat to vegetables to be able to enjoy the green curry.

The last must have when you visit Thailand is the popular mango sticky rice dessert. It is among the favorites in the country by tourists and locals alike. It is even featured in some cooking shows and food exhibits.

The mango sticky rice is made with sweetened coconut milk. A ripe mango is then placed on top of the sticky rice. Meanwhile, this dessert is made into bite sized balls in some restaurants, topped with sweet sauce.

Visitors coming to Thailand need not to worry about food prices as these are really cheap. You can spend $4 for a day's meal including some snacks and drinks. Foreigners who settle in Thailand for the first time are often surprised with cost of an apartment. You can get one rented in downtown Bangkok for a cheap rate of $300 per month. Aside from that, you won't find it difficult to look for food as there will always be a food kiosk available on the side of the road. Plus, you get a great value for the money you pay!

Chapter VII: Must See Festivals and Events

Everyone loves festivals and events and you will not be disappointed as Thailand offers a lot of festivities to enjoy. These festivals in the country are celebrated to show the rich culture and enthusiasm of its people. The Songkran is ideal for those who love water. It is celebrated every 13th of April in mostly every city in the country. However, it is much celebrated in Bangkok where people enjoy water fights. You will be able to see soaking wet people walking on the streets and those who are looking forward to getting soaked. Water symbolizes cleansing and this is the main reason why Thais celebrate this event. It is also believed to be a good start for the new year among people in Thailand.

Loei Province in Isan also holds a festival called Phi Ta Khon, the feast of the ghosts. It is a religious event showcasing the beliefs of locals with regards to spirits and ghost. This is also comparable to the Halloween celebration of westerners. The event takes place between June and July and is regarded to be the most colorful. Dancing and merry making is rampant along the streets. Men are dressed in colorful costumes and masked as spirits.

Those who love animals will surely enjoy the bizarre festival celebrated in the town of Lopburi. A buffet of food in honor of monkeys is given to feed the animals. This happens every last Sunday of November. You will enjoy watching monkeys eat while taking photographs together with them.

Another beautiful celebration to watch out for is the Loi Krathong. This is celebrated during the 12th lunar month when the moon is at its fullest. People believe that their wishes could be granted during this time. They would light candles and have it float in their local rivers. The lighted waters truly make a magnificent scene.

Meanwhile, the start of the Buddhist Lenten festival in Thailand is celebrated with the Ubon Ratchatani Candle festival. More than 70 wax figures are paraded on the streets that gets audience amazed. If you are planning to visit Chiang Mai, make sure you book somewhere near the last week of February. This will enable you to catch the Flower Festival where floral parade highlights the event. Beauty contests, handicrafts on sale and an exhibit of flowers are also held during the festival.

The Festival of the Crystal Sons, otherwise known as Poy Sang Long, is celebrated from March to April. This is celebrated among the Tai Yai people wherein a novice ordination is held and believed to be giving them more advantage compared to the regular Buddhist ordination.

The rural village of Hat Siao celebrates the Hat Siao Elephant Ordination festival every 7th day of April. During the celebration, elephants are dressed in colorful costumes and are paraded on the streets where novice devotees of Buddhism are seated on their backs for ordination. The inspiration for this event came from the legend of Vessandorn, wherein the elephant Patchainakhen ensured there would be enough rain at the time of Buddha's incarnation was born.

By May, you would be able to catch the celebration of the Visakha Bucha. At this time, the holiest of the Buddhist religion is celebrated making most of the temples in the country jampacked. Still in May, locals celebrated the Bu Bun Fai wherein rockets are launched in different sizes. They believe that this will guarantee a plenty harvest for the next season of planting rice.

During the full moon in July, the Khao Pansa is celebrated to mark the start of the Buddhist retreat. This is the time wherein monks return to the temples to fulfill their religious obligations for a period of 3 months. This is also the time when Thai men seek to enter monkhood.

If you are a vegetarian, visiting Thailand will surely get you delighted. This is because the a feast for vegetarians is held in Phuket mainly to honor those who have Chinese ancestry. This occurs during the early weeks of October. Chinese temples are often full and a vegetarian diet that lasts for 10 days is observed. Still in the month of October, visitors will be able to witness the Chonburi Buffalo races. Buffaloes have been a great part of the Thai culture and this festival is celebrated in their owner. Beauty contests are also held as part of the festival that often attracts more people to come and watch.

Visitors taking a trip to Thailand by late November to December will be able to witness the Kanchanaburi. You can experience having a ride on vintage trains during this time and can also witness exhibits themed on history and archaeology. The River Kwai is the venue for this celebration which is highlighted by a sound and lights presentation.

Another festival celebrated in the country is the Ayuthaya festival held in December. A cultural exhibit is displayed showing the rich heritage of the region. There are also performances and cultural parades being held along with light and sound exhibitions. In
1991, UNESCO has declared Ayuthaya a world heritage site.

The Royal Barge celebration is another event to watch out for but this only happens on special occasions. During this time, the procession would go along the Chao Phraya River in Bangkok. The procession of the Royal Barge usually takes about an hour to be able to journey on the river. Spectators can see different amazing sights including historical barges escorted by numerous boats. Some bridges are also partly closed while restrictions on the places for regular ferries and boats are also done.

Meanwhile, those who are planning to spend their holidays in Thailand can experience the Hat Yai Lantern Fest in Hat Yai region. This is when they celebrate the "colors of the south" festival and has been regarded to be one of the most colorful events in the country. The celebration runs from November until February.

Most of the festivals and events in Thailand are centered towards the Buddhist religion. Even if you are not Buddhist, believers would still welcome you to watch and enjoy their religious celebrations. Celebrations are held annually ensuring that you can always come back the following year in case a festival has already been celebrated.

Thailand is a country full of foreigners mingling with the locals. Most of the foreigners visiting the land of smiles come from New Zealand, Japan, Germany, Argentina, Israel, France and Australia. It is also gaining popularity to most tourists coming from the United States. The country is also a top choice for backpackers and adventure seekers.

You would not find it hard to go around the city should you wish to visit during the months where festivals are celebrated. It is also a convenient place because you can simply buy food in almost every street as there will always be a food cart situated. This will keep your stomachs full while watching or joining a festival. You also don't have to worry about coming home late nights or getting hungry even at 3 AM as there will always be available street foods.

See You In Thailand!

We hope you enjoyed this travel guide to Thailand! After exploring all of the wonderful things Thailand has to offer in this book, we hope that we have provided lots of inspiration as you plan your journey. Safe and happy travels, or as they say in Thailand, "tîeow hâi sà-nùk"!

Experience Everything Travel Guide Collection™

73834379R00026

Made in the USA
Lexington, KY
12 December 2017